Essen

MW00454433

Teachers

Teachers deal with change on a regular basis, but there are some principles at the core of teaching that remain constant and that have the biggest impact on student achievement. In this inspiring book from Danny Steele, creator of the popular Steele Thoughts blog, and Todd Whitaker, bestselling author and speaker, you'll learn how to focus on the most important things in the classroom, not just the "current" things. The authors reveal essential truths that will make you a more effective educator in areas such as student relationships, classroom management, and classroom culture. The strategies are presented in digestible chunks, perfect for book studies, in-service sessions, mentorship meetings, and other learning formats. With the inspiring anecdotes and insights in this book, you'll be reminded of your greater purpose – making a difference in students' lives.

Danny Steele (@steelethoughts) is a principal from Birmingham, Alabama and has worked in public education for over 25 years. In 2016, he was named Alabama's Secondary Principal of the Year. He has presented at numerous state and national conferences, and he serves as an adjunct instructor at the University of Montevallo. Danny writes an educational leadership blog that has received over 5 million page views.

Todd Whitaker (@toddwhitaker) is a professor of educational leadership at the University of Missouri. He is a leading presenter in the field of education and has written more than 50 books, including the national bestsellers *What Great Teachers Do Differently* and *Your First Year: How to Survive and Thrive as a New Teacher*, co-written with Madeline Whitaker and Katherine Whitaker.

Also Available from Routledge Eye On Education

www.routledge.com/eyeoneducation

Essential Truths for Principals
Danny Steele and Todd Whitaker

Your First Year: How to Survive and Thrive as a New Teacher
Todd Whitaker, Madeline Whitaker, and Katherine Whitaker

Classroom Management from the Ground Up
Todd Whitaker, Madeline Whitaker Good, and Katherine Whitaker

What Great Teachers Do Differently, 2nd Edition: 17 Things That Matter Most
Todd Whitaker

What Connected Educators Do Differently
Todd Whitaker, Jeffrey Zoul, and Jimmy Casas

Dealing with Difficult Parents, 2nd Edition
Todd Whitaker and Douglas J. Fiore

Study Guide to Dealing with Difficult Parents
Todd Whitaker and Douglas J. Fiore

Leading School Change, 2nd Edition: How to Overcome Resistance, Increase Buy-In, and Accomplish Your Goals
Todd Whitaker

Teaching Matters, 2nd Edition: How to Keep Your Passion and Thrive in Today's Classroom
Todd Whitaker and Beth Whitaker

Essential Truths for Teachers

Danny Steele and Todd Whitaker

Routledge
Taylor & Francis Group

NEW YORK AND LONDON

First published 2019
by Routledge
52 Vanderbilt Avenue, New York, NY 10017

and by Routledge
2 Park Square, Milton Park, Abingdon, Oxon, OX14 4RN

Routledge is an imprint of the Taylor & Francis Group, an informa business

Library of Congress Cataloging-in-Publication Data
Names: Steele, Danny, author. | Whitaker, Todd, 1959- author.
Title: Essential truths for teachers / Danny Steele and Todd Whitaker.
Description: New York : Routledge, 2019.
Identifiers: LCCN 2018041792 (print) | LCCN 2018045639 (ebook) |
ISBN 9780429022029 (ebook) | ISBN 9780367076788 (hbk) | ISBN
9780367076795 (pbk) | ISBN 9780429022029 (ebk)
Subjects: LCSH: Teacher effectiveness. | Teacher-student relationships. |
Classroom management. | Classroom environment. | Teaching–
Anecdotes.
Classification: LCC LB1025.3 (ebook) | LCC LB1025.3 .S7343 2019
(print) | DDC 371.102–dc23
LC record available at https://lccn.loc.gov/2018041792

ISBN: 978-0-367-07678-8 (hbk)
ISBN: 978-0-367-07679-5 (pbk)
ISBN: 978-0-429-02202-9 (ebk)

Typeset in Palatino
by Swales & Willis Ltd, Exeter, Devon, UK

For the many passionate teachers I have worked with over the years – you have inspired me. Thank you for caring about students.

Danny

This book is dedicated to our grandson, Tapley.

Todd

Contents

Meet the Authors

Dr. Danny Steele is a principal from Birmingham, Alabama, and has worked in public education for over 25 years. In addition to serving as a principal at multiple levels, he has worked as a teacher, coach, and assistant principal. In 2005, Danny was recognized as the Secondary Assistant Principal of the Year for the state of Alabama, and in 2016 he was named Alabama's Secondary Principal of the Year. He has presented at numerous state and national conferences. He serves as an adjunct instructor at the University of Montevallo (AL), and writes an educational leadership blog that has received over 5 million page views. Danny has an undergraduate degree in History from Covenant College (Lookout Mountain, GA); he has an M.A. in History from the University of Alabama (Birmingham); he has an Educational Specialist degree in Educational Administration and an Educational Doctorate degree in Educational Leadership – both from Samford University (Birmingham, AL). He lives with his wife, Holley, in Birmingham, Alabama. They have three children: DJ, Will, and Elizabeth.

Dr. Todd Whitaker is a professor of educational leadership at the University of Missouri, Columbia, and professor emeritus at Indiana State University, Terre Haute. Prior to moving into higher education he was a math teacher and basketball coach in Missouri. Todd then served as a principal at the middle school, junior high, and high school levels. He was also a middle school coordinator in charge of staffing, curriculum, and technology for the opening of new middle schools. He has spent his life pursuing his love of education by researching and studying effective teachers and principals.

One of the nation's leading authorities on staff motivation, leading change, and teacher and principal effectiveness, Todd has written over 50 books, including the national bestseller, *What Great Teachers Do Differently*. Other titles include: *Your First Year, Shifting The Monkey, Dealing With Difficult Teachers, The Ten-Minute Inservice, The Ball, What Great Principals Do Differently, Motivating & Inspiring Teachers*, and *Dealing With Difficult Parents*.

Todd is married to Beth, also a former teacher and principal, who is a professor of Educational Leadership at the University of Missouri. They are the parents of three children: Katherine, Madeline, and Harrison.

Preface

Programs and initiatives come and go so regularly in education that it becomes difficult to determine what to focus on next. Seemingly every year/month/week/day there are increasing demands on teachers and principals to do the next "great" thing that will change the world. Some of these things are positive and others not so much. Amazingly, many of them – and even some of the positive ones – tend to disappear into the air like a fine mist. What was labeled as the most important thing in the world disappears into an afterthought. This revolving door of change can result in a furrowed brow or a cynical frown at what comes next. It is so easy to feel the demands and pressures of standardized testing, increasing accountability, and expanding expectations on all of us. It is easy to fall into the "what's next" trap or even the "is it all worth it?" mind set. This is quite natural as the pressure continues to mount. It may even lead to hopelessness. Is there nothing that is constant that we can rely on for guidance? Are we just continually adrift at sea, eyeing the next storm?

However, everyone – educators and non-educators alike – can look back to their schooling and reflect on things learned that have not disappeared from our memories. Some of them are light and fun. Others we may not remember with the same degree of fondness. Yet some of the most indelible memories surround the teachers that made an imprint on our minds, hearts, and souls, and forever changed us. We may not remember the textbook, or the curriculum from that class, and yet there is a piece of us that will never forget the lessons we learned from the teacher. We can probably remember how the classroom looked, what the tone in the room was like, the facial expressions of the teacher – maybe even what they wore and their mannerisms. And, maybe we cannot recall those details. But without a doubt we can remember how we *felt* as a student in that setting.

It may make us smile, it may make us feel intellectually challenged, it may make us chuckle. But there was something special about that teacher that years later still resonates inside of us. Just think, if every teacher we had resulted in that much of an impact, how would our life be different?

We do not think back and say, "It's a shame they didn't have technology then", or, "I wish they had infused project-based learning into their curriculum." Instead we reflect with amazement at what they did and how they did it. Many of us wish we could feel that way again and have teachers and others that impact our lives in that fashion. Most educators can name teachers they had that have influenced them and may hope that they can have the same impact on their own students. Well, we believe every teacher can have this kind of an impact.

Not only can educators look back fondly on teachers they had, they can often reflect on experiences in their own classroom as a teacher where they felt immense pride in their connections with their students and the learning that was taking place in their class. What was different about those days? We can also probably recall the butterflies of our first ever day of teaching and the excitement of the first day of school each year. How can we keep that going? Or how can we reignite that feeling during tougher stretches of the year, or when we have particularly challenging classrooms?

Discipline plans come and go, changes in technology can make us feel like a stranger in our own classroom, and choosing from the range of instructional strategies can seem like drinking from a fire hose. Is there anything that is at the core of teaching that everyone can rely on? What is it that really matters most?

Despite the changes that are occurring like a whipsaw, there are some constants that educators can know will always be there. There are things that provide an impact whether we work with preschoolers or high school seniors. There are ways to teach that will reach the most challenging students now and in the future. Rather than trying to do the current things, we must all strive to do the important things.

This book is designed to help us find and do the things in education that have a permanent shelf life. Those things, and the people that do them, are much more long-ranging than many fads that come and go in education. Whether we are in our first year or forty-first year we all want to make a difference. That's why we chose education. To influence and improve the lives of our students. Here is our chance. Educators are at their best when they operate from their core – when they go through their day mindful of the values that drive them. Whether this book alters the path you are on or gives you the confidence to accelerate on your current road, our purpose is to remind us why we chose education, and to become the teacher that students remember forever.

How to Use This Book

Our goal is to provide a book that you can use when you most need it. You can sit down and devour it like a traditional book, front-to-back. You might want to highlight or dog-ear parts that resonate for later reading. Maybe you want to start off your Monday, or every day, looking for a new idea or much-needed reminder. Maybe it is a book you want to share with your colleagues or use as a gift for teacher friends. A school may want to pass it around from person to person, having someone identify something that a colleague does well. This could be reinforced by putting a sticky-note on a page and sharing why it reminded them of this person. Maybe you can reflect on a quote at the beginning of a faculty meeting. There is no limit to the possibilities.

But the real purpose of this book is to make a difference – to help us remember why we chose education and to align our long-held beliefs with our current practices. There are many things in education we cannot control. However, there are many things that we *can* control every day. Let's get started.

Essential Truths

1

When Teachers Love Their Jobs, Students Notice. When Teachers Are Counting Down the Days, Students Notice. It Turns Out, Students Notice a Lot!

We all give off vibes, and in the classroom, it's not hard for students to pick up on the vibes of the teacher. The students notice if teachers are in a good mood or a bad mood. They notice if they are enjoying the day or if the day seems like drudgery. They notice when the teacher is exasperated. And make no mistake, the energy projected by the teacher will affect the energy that the students bring to the lesson. The positive energy of the teacher is the single most important factor in determining the climate of the classroom. When teachers realize their own attitude affects the motivation of their students, it can be a game changer.

The best teachers don't show up for "work," they show up for the kids. It's not just a job ... it's a passion. And their passion will define them more than any lesson plan. The students will more than likely remember that passion longer than any lesson. They may not remember what their teachers taught them, but they will always remember if their teachers enjoyed teaching them.

2

You Never Know What Students Are Dealing with at Home. Always Be Kind. Always Be Patient. Always Be Gracious. Always.

I remember when Demetrius was in my office – the principal's office – seated next to his mother. He was there because he had "jumped" another boy in the locker room. I was in the process of assigning him several days of in-school suspension, and wanted his mother to be aware of what we were dealing with. At one point in the meeting, Demetrius started to explain himself to me. He had barely opened his mouth long enough to get out two words when his mother popped him in the face with her hand. She did not even appear to look at him. It happened so fast, it startled both of us. I do not recall much of a reaction from Demetrius, other than being startled and a bit embarrassed (I think the physical pain from the slap was minor compared with his humiliation). He continued looking forward the entire time. This happened many years ago. It was my sense that this was not an unusual occurrence. As Demetrius and I were walking down the sidewalk to in-school suspension, I remember saying to him something like, "I'm sorry that happened, Demetrius. Nobody should have to deal with that." And I remember thinking to myself, "This guy doesn't have a chance. No wonder he's slapping other kids in the locker room. Violence is what he knows."

Many teachers have had the experience of scheduling a parent conference to discuss the failure of a student completing homework, only to have the parent not show up for the conference. I have called home to discuss a child's disrespectful attitude, only to have the parent berate me on the telephone. Make no mistake about it: Students are products of their environment.

It is nice to think about students coming to school with a "blank slate," and it is nice to imagine that education is the process where teachers get to write on that clean slate with everything children need to be productive citizens. It is a rewarding profession, when teachers mold the lives of young students and get to paint a beautiful picture on the canvas of their lives. But here is the thing: The kids never come with a blank slate, and teachers are not the only ones painting on the canvas. Much has been written about the advantages enjoyed by kindergartners who had parents read to them in the first 5 years of their lives. The advantages of these kids extend beyond vocabulary acquisition, and they certainly do not stop at kindergarten. Likewise, the challenges that confront students who do not come from a supportive home environment remain with them throughout their schooling career. Some students come into our classes with values and habits already instilled in them that are counterproductive to those we are trying to instill. And, when they go home each day, they are often receiving messages that undermine what we are trying to accomplish in the classroom.

So what does this mean for educators? It does not mean that we lower our standards, and it does not mean that we whine about lack of parental support. It *does* mean that we remain aware of the challenges that some of our students are having to overcome. It *does* mean that we have to provide additional support, instruction, and even coaching in areas that might extend beyond traditional curricular standards. And it certainly means that we practice empathy – that we extend grace and compassion to every one of our students. Some students need us to be their cheerleader more than they need us to be their instructor.

> " Some students need us to be their cheerleader more than they need us to be their instructor. "

The next time you are frustrated with a student in your class, think about what that student's canvas looked like before they came to you ... and think about who might be writing on it after the bell rings. After all, we don't always know what our students came from – or what they're going home to. When you find out about the home life of some of your students, it will change your attitude and your approach toward those students. It must.

3

When Teachers Are In It for the Students, They Are Not as Quick to Complain about Minor Issues.

Students sometimes act immature. Sometimes they are too silly. Sometimes they fidget too much. Our students are sometimes preoccupied with ridiculous things. And kids sometimes do unexpectedly ridiculous things in class. They shouldn't, but they do. It is so significant when teachers do not sweat the minor misbehaviors. It makes such a difference when teachers look at things from the students' perspective. After all, some things that drive adults crazy capture the imagination of the students. It is greatly appreciated when teachers do not allow minor annoyances to distract them from the number one priority: Teaching students and building relationships with them.

4

Student Engagement Is Usually in Direct Proportion to Teacher Enthusiasm.

I remember seeing a sign in my dentist's office that read, "You don't have to floss all your teeth – just the ones you want to keep." I have thought about making a sign for my office that reads, "Teachers don't have to care about all their lessons – just the lessons they want their students to learn." What students find most compelling in a classroom, is usually not the brilliantly scaffolded lesson, and it's certainly not the dry textbook, it's the energy, attitude, and enthusiasm of the teacher. Students are not motivated by lessons; they are motivated by teachers. My most memorable teacher – the one who motivated me – was Mr. Navarre. He taught me Earth Science when I was in the eighth grade. I learned to love rocks when I was 13 years old, and I still own the rock box that I constructed that year. I loved rocks because Mr. Navarre loved rocks. His passion inspired me. As teachers, it is unreasonable for us to expect students to engage in our lesson when we're not that excited about teaching it. But on the flip side, genuine enthusiasm from the teacher can make almost any lesson engaging. Ultimately, what is most engaging to the students, is not the lesson, it's the enthusiasm of the teacher.

5

Don't Assume Your Students Know You Care about Them. You Gotta Show Them . . . Every Day.

There is a well-known saying that every reader is familiar with: "Actions speak louder than words." It is well worn because it resonates with all of us.

Students don't know their teachers care about them because it said so on the syllabus or because the teacher routinely proclaims to the entire class: "You guys know how much I love you." Students know their teacher cares about them by how they treat them. They can't say it; they have to show it. When you talk to your students outside of your classroom, you show it. When your students are having a bad day and you demonstrate compassion, you show it. When they lose a loved one and you call and check on them, or maybe even visit them, you show it.

As teachers, we don't ever want our students wondering if we care about them. We need our actions to leave no room for doubt.

6

If You Start Treating Your Most Challenging Students as If They Are Your Favorite Students, Over Time They Might Start Acting Like Your Favorites.

There is an element of the "self-fulfilling prophecy" that plays out in teacher–student relationships. Our attitude toward students will affect the way we interact with them in subtle and not-so-subtle ways. When we are aggravated with a student, we are a little more irritable with them, a little less patient, and a little less gracious. On the flip side, we are extraordinarily patient and flexible with our favorite students. We always give them the benefit of the doubt. When teachers begin extending those same courtesies to the challenging students, they often notice that those students respond positively. Students rise and fall to our expectations. The student that seemingly always gets on our last nerve may actually have a lot of potential. That is what we must remind ourselves of. That is what we must focus on. When we look for good qualities, we can surprise ourselves with how many we find.

7

Good Lesson Plans Don't Redeem Poor Relationships. Get to Know Your Students ... Then It Becomes Much Easier to Teach Them.

There was a student named Mario who was always in trouble and was always in the office. In particular, he was constantly being written up by Ms. Johnson. I assigned Mario to detention, I assigned him in-school suspension, and, at times, I even assigned him full-suspension. As often as he was in my office, he received a lot of discipline from me. But he and I had a great relationship. For years I have had a picture of Michael Jordan in my office. Mario loved basketball, and virtually every time he was in my office, he asked if he could have that poster of Jordan. His dream was to make the JV basketball team. He wasn't quite 5-feet tall in the ninth grade, and from what I could tell, didn't have a lot of ability ... but basketball was his passion. So, we would talk about basketball. By about February of that year, Ms. Johnson came to me, and she was at her wit's end. She exclaimed, "I just don't know what to do with Mario! Do you have any suggestions?" I responded, "Ms. Johnson, do you know what Mario's dream is?" She didn't. I went on, "Ms. Johnson, Mario's dream is to make the JV basketball team." I suggested to her that she take some time to get to know Mario – to connect with him on a personal level.

The teachers who have the biggest impact on kids practice empathy. They don't just teach their students; they try to understand them. I know a lot of teachers have students fill out personal information on the first day of school. That's a great practice, but we have to use the information that the students tell us. It gives us a window into their world. It can provide the groundwork for developing a relationship. If you want students to take an interest in your class, start by taking an interest in them. When students feel a connection to their teacher they are much more likely to care about the lesson. And when they have a good relationship with their teacher they are always less likely to act out in class. If Ms. Johnson understood and appreciated Mario's dream in September, it's possible her entire year could have gone differently. It's good for teachers to know their content, and it's great for them to know the pedagogy, but it's imperative for them to know the kids.

> **"The teachers who have the biggest impact on kids practice empathy."**

8

The Best Teachers Figure Out How to Handle Their Frustrations without Complaining – They Have Challenges, but They Don't Dwell in Negativity.

All teachers are confronted with challenges during the day; they all face circumstances that could be discouraging. But good educators are not victims of unfair mandates, unruly kids, or unsupportive parents. They are change agents and they rise above the adversity. Many of the challenging circumstances are out of the teacher's control. Teachers cannot control the parents, the mandates, or the class size. They *can* control their quality of instruction and the passion they bring into their classroom. Good teachers realize that they can control their own attitude. They choose to focus on what is positive. They remain mindful of the role that they play in the classroom, and they never forget their potential for impacting students. It is in fact possible to see the glass as being half-full. That's what good teachers try and do. All teachers have bad days, and all teachers need to vent from time to time. Great teachers keep things in perspective.

9

When You See a Teacher Interact with a Challenging Student, You May Not Learn Much about the Student, but You Will Learn Plenty about the Teacher.

Every school in America has challenging students, and virtually every teacher in our schools is confronted with these students at some point during the day. Some of them are challenging because they never come to class prepared. Some are challenging because they can't sit still. Some are challenging because they always seem to have a chip on their shoulder. Some are challenging because of their disrespectful attitude. And then some students are challenging because they just don't seem to care about anything.

But here's the thing, while there are teachers at every school who complain about these students at the lunch table or in the teacher's lounge, those schools have teachers who experience success with those same students. Those students are a thorn in the side of the first group of teachers, yet they are a source of professional satisfaction with the second group. So what is the difference?

Some teachers realize the student who never comes to class prepared might not have a lot of support at home.

Maybe the student is disorganized and irresponsible, but when the student shows up without a pencil, they give them a pencil. They don't make a thing of it because they realize there are better ways to teach responsibility. And they certainly do not want anything to be a barrier to class participation.

Some teachers realize that the student who cannot sit still does not like getting in trouble; he just has an over-abundance of energy. (I know adults who can't sit still for forty-five minutes, and I bet you do too.) I had a teacher who made a deal with one of these students that he could stand up to do his work as long as he got it done. The deal worked like magic.

Some teachers realize that the student with a chip on their shoulder has had a miserable school experience. They haven't found anything they feel good about in school so they don't have healthy ways of getting attention. Those teachers go out of their way to show respect to these students and affirm them as often as possible. They do not engage in petty "battles" in the classroom because they understand that when there is a battle in the classroom, nobody wins.

Some teachers realize that the student's disrespectful attitude likely has nothing to do with the teacher. They do not lower their standards, but they also do not take everything personally. These teachers work to build positive rapport on the first day of school, so antagonistic attitudes never even take root.

Some teachers realize that the students who do not seem to care about anything may not be as apathetic as they seem. These teachers have a conviction that no student wants to fail, no student likes being in trouble, and no student wants to be labeled a "loser." They recognize that every student cares about something, but maybe the adults in the building just have not figured out what it is or how to cultivate it. Maybe these students just do not see the relevance of school, so these teachers work harder to make their class meaningful. Maybe these students are tired of not being good enough at school; they find that not trying is preferable to encountering failure yet again. It can be a shield to protect themselves from embarrassment. So these teachers are relentless about supporting the students and finding little ways for them to experience success. They know that the little successes can eventually turn into big successes.

Great teachers recognize that the challenging students are the ones that need them the most. The best teachers are never victims of "slacker" kids. They refuse to let those students get away without doing the work. These teachers got into education to make a difference in the lives of these kids. They are able to look past the frustrating behaviors and see the potential.

> "Great teachers recognize that the challenging students are the ones that need them the most."

10

It Is Not the Hours that Make Teaching so Challenging, It Is the Intensity.

Teaching, coaching, and principaling are incredibly difficult jobs. There are long hours and many times our jobs carry over way past our "contract time." This is a given in education. However, what makes our job so challenging is not the hours, it is the intensity. We care so much, we give so much, we try so hard. We all wonder, "What is an uninterrupted lunch?" We reflect on the myriad of decisions we make each day and how they all impacted the people we worked with. We wonder if we were patient enough with one situation and too patient with another. We worry that we were too quick to issue consequences at 9:30 and not quick enough at 2:00.

If we go into a store or watch a show on television we wonder how the things we see can be utilized in our classrooms. It is very difficult to turn off our minds and hearts. This is one reason you are so good. The best people do carry these thoughts with them. They are continually looking through their educator lens. But at the same time we have to figure out a way to take care of ourselves. That is why teachers need regular breaks. Our summers off aren't even really off, but without that we would never wind down and recoup our energy. You are not really working 9 months a year when you put 12 months of energy into the 9 you have with students.

Please make sure that you take care of yourself. The students deserve the best you. And so does your family.

11

We Are Not in the Perfection Business, We Are in the Improvement Business.

One challenge that many outstanding teachers have is that they compare themselves to perfection. People who are less successful often compare everyone else to perfection. However, in education there is no perfection. We are working with young people. We are continually working to move in the right direction but, unfortunately, we never really arrive at a fixed destination. What you do in the classroom is incredible and you are always building and growing something better. But if we are looking for perfection we will never reach it.

With a student who is behaviorally challenged (do you like that term?) we have to look for a trend-line rather than a definitive point. Are they on task more often now than earlier in the year? Do they seem to be better at peer relations in March than January?

We may feel at times that our class is completely out of control, but when we look at the most respectful students we realize that it isn't all students, it is some students. This can help us center on what we have done right – which is often a great deal – versus what we have done wrong or still need to accomplish.

Holding yourself to a standard of perfection is pretty tough. Thinking of our students through that lens is clearly a no-win situation. Enjoy the small steps, the directional shifts, and allow for these celebrations. You do make a difference. Just remember, it is sometimes the direction we are going rather than the pace of the journey that makes the trip worthwhile.

12

Some Students Have Taller Mountains to Climb than Others. We Can't Climb the Mountains for Them, but an Awareness of the Mountains Reminds Us of the Importance of Our Patience and Support.

Many years ago, when I was a first-year assistant principal, I remember being frustrated with a 16-year-old boy named Cedric. He was defiant, belligerent, and seemed to have no respect for authority. He always had a chip on his shoulder and had no trouble maintaining his tough image with me. He was what we called "hard." I prided myself on building relationships with students, but I could not ever get him to let down his guard. I had run out of patience with him, and I confess that I had sort of written him off. One day in my office, I decided to give it another go. I said, "Cedric, we all have challenges in life; we all have mountains that we have to climb. What challenges do you have in your life?" I was not prepared for what he told me. Cedric's demeanor became a little softer as he said, "I don't have anyone to take care of me." This is a moment I will never forget.

Cedric lived with his 80-year-old invalid grandmother and she was not able to do much. She certainly was unable to provide the kind of support, guidance, and supervision that 16-year-olds need. I had been upset with this kid for skipping class to play basketball and then being disrespectful when he was caught. As I sat in my office listening to him describe his home situation, I thought to myself, "How is this guy even showing up to school?"

I sometimes think about Cedric, and wonder how he is doing. I only worked in that school for 1 year, so I have not seen him since then. I know that guy had the deck stacked against him, though. I wish all of his teachers knew his story. Every student has a "story," and some of those stories will break your heart. Many students have a hard home life … and, sometimes, that shows up as a bad attitude at school. Teachers cannot fix the home situation, but I am grateful for the ones who are understanding and patient. There is always something going on behind that "bad attitude."

13

It's Good When Teachers Criticize Privately and Praise Publicly. These Teachers Usually Have Better Class Climates.

When you understand Maslow's Hierarchy of Needs, you realize that embarrassing a student is not a good idea, because more than likely, their reputation with other students is the most important thing to them. Embarrassing students puts them in a position where they feel compelled to "save face," and it often escalates a classroom issue from something petty to behavior that is disrespectful or defiant. When a student is disrespectful, it is usually not about the teacher. It's usually about the other students who are watching. When you have to address a problem behavior, a great idea is whispering to the student. This avoids the embarrassment and the potential verbal retaliation.

Conversely, praising students publicly generates positive energy in the classroom. It boosts the esteem of whomever is being bragged on, and it reinforces for the students what is valued in the classroom. Never underestimate the value of positive reinforcement, and remember that it is usually more meaningful when it is public. There is more to effective instruction than delivering a good lesson. Never forget that a good class climate is essential for good learning.

14

Great Teachers Always Come to Class Ready to Teach, but They Are Mindful of the Fact that Not All Students Come to Class Ready to Learn.

Good teachers plan, and really good teachers overplan. These teachers always come to class prepared to teach. Great teachers are ready to teach too, but they realize all of their students do not walk in the door at the same place – academically, socially, or emotionally. Students come to school with "baggage." The best teachers do not just teach good lessons, they understand the baggage, and they account for this dynamic as they are delivering instruction and interacting with students. Maybe one student was tripped in the hallway by some bigger boys who thought it was funny. He is preoccupied during class thinking about how he can avoid those kids walking to his next class. Another student was up much of the night listening to her parents argue, so she is continually dozing off in class. Another student did not have anyone at home to help him with his homework, so he walks into class feeling embarrassed and behind. As teachers, we would like to think that our lesson is the most important thing to the student. In reality, everything else in the student's world trumps the lesson. We should always remember that every student walks into our class with a unique set of circumstances – their own struggles and challenges. Great teachers are sensitive to the needs of their students. They bring empathy, patience, and kindness to their classroom. They create a safe place for students, and this creates a more effective learning environment.

15

Very Seldom Do the Loudest Barks Come from the Smartest Dogs.

There is an old saying that the squeaky wheel gets the grease. Well, if it fixes the problem then that probably is a good thing. However, when it comes to working with students or colleagues, sometimes giving attention to someone who is regularly complaining does not actually solve the problem. It may just reinforce it.

We would estimate that over 90 percent of student misbehavior is because they want attention. Ironically, the same reality is true of adult misbehavior. Everyone wants attention. We have to realize that someone saying something in a brazen tone or sending an email with ALL CAPS and plenty of !!!! does not mean that they are correct. It does not even mean they have confidence. Sometimes it demonstrates insecurity more than anything else.

We have to remember to trust our instincts as a teacher. Just because others state their opinion doesn't mean they are right or wrong. No one knows your class and your style better than you. If every teacher "trusted their gut" students would be treated with respect a lot more often. Think about it. The first time a teacher was rude or yelled at a student there is a great chance that they felt uncomfortable. They felt like they did something wrong. If they relied on their core senses they would reflect and work to never do it again. However, if they happen to hear other teachers do these things – or even hear teachers brag about doing these things – they may ignore that inner voice. If we continue to do these things we eventually lose our way because we get used to feeling uncomfortable and these behaviors become normalized.

If we have ever worked with a negative person we may have seen them challenge peers who are happy and smiling. Have you ever heard a less than perky colleague say to a co-worker, "What are you smiling at?"; "Why are you so happy?"; "Why do you come to work so early or stay so late?" If we let these voices be the ones we respond to we may end up being less positive, productive, and effective.

Trust your instincts. The students need the best of you. The real you.

16

Some Students Dream of Trying to Change the World – and Some Students Are Just Trying to Make It through the Day. The Best Teachers Meet the Students Right Where They Are.

One of my favorite things about our school is the "Wall of Dreams." For the last few years, we have asked all of our students to write their dream on a 16-foot whiteboard that we have hung in the hallway. I love showing off our special wall to visitors in the building, and it is always a powerful experience when they see it for the first time. I want them to see the hopes, goals, and aspirations of the awesome students in our school. I also love for teachers to walk past this wall and be reminded of their "WHY." We certainly want to raise student achievement in our school, but that is not why we became educators. We are mindful that students are much more than a test score. We want to make a difference for students. We want to inspire them

> **"**We certainly want to raise student achievement in our school, but that is not why we became educators.**"**

and empower them to chase their dreams and reach their potential. The students walking the halls of our schools have a variety of dreams. These are some of the ones that our students have written:

> *"To be a sixth-grade Peer Helper."*
> *"To be a loving mother."*
> *"To be better at math."*
> *"I want to be happy."*
> *"My dream is for my sister to get out of the Air Force alive."*
> *"To be a kindergarten teacher."*
> *"To get a college scholarship."*
> *"I want to do something that MEANS something."*

As educators, we are inspiring students to chase their dreams. It's important to recognize, however, that students' hopes and dreams can take many different forms. And sometimes, what our students need most is for us to be their cheerleader – to instill in them the confidence that they can do it!

17

Provoking One Good Question Can Be Better than Giving Ten Right Answers.

Many teachers give too many answers to students who are not even asking questions. The best teachers cultivate curiosity. Which professional learning opportunities are teachers most interested in? The answer is simple: Teachers are interested in the ones that they choose. And they choose them because they think they have a need in that area. They choose the professional learning sessions that will provide information that they want to understand, or will provide skills for which they see the need.

Many of us have experienced faculty meetings where some teachers only started listening when they thought something was being addressed that they needed to know ... or wanted to know. Most students learn the same way as adults. They pay closer attention to the teacher when the teacher is talking about something that seems relevant to them – when they are answering questions that the students are asking. The best learning happens when students are pursuing answers to their own questions. Schools can compel the attendance of students, but teachers must understand that the learning is always voluntary. This realization must drive teachers to make the classroom experience relevant to the students.

18

Effective Teachers Do Not Have to Prove Who Is in Charge; Everybody Knows Who Is in Charge – And the More We Try to Prove It, the More the Students Try to Prove Us Wrong.

We often hear about "demanding" authority and "earning" respect. You may know how to do these two things, but I do not. We are blessed. We do not have to earn respect. The students give it to us. Think what students are like the first day of school. They are often hesitant, cooperative, maybe even nervous. They are compliant. We did not earn that. It was a gift they have given us. Now the question is what do we do with it? Some teachers cultivate it, and help it grow all year. Others may begin to lose that respect within the first few weeks.

The very best teachers do not have to "prove" who is in charge. The students all know it. And when teachers try to prove it the students work very hard at trying to prove them wrong. No one, regardless of age or point in life, likes to be told what to do. When a teacher threatens "I don't want to hear a peep" most of us have an incredible urge to let out a loud "peep!!" before our head explodes.

Teachers with strong classroom management do not have to remind students who the adult is in the classroom. The students begin to figure that out the first day of school.

> **"**Teachers with strong classroom management do not have to remind students who the adult is in the classroom.**"**

Students give us that gift and the best teachers nurture it all year. They build on the initial respect and do things *with* the students rather than *to* the students. In every situation in a classroom we hope that there is at least one adult. And it works best if it happens to be the teacher.

19

Teachers Never Have to Say Something Mean, They Just Have to Mean What They Say.

We have seen coaches who yell at their players. We have also seen coaches who do not. What is amazing is these coaches may not differ in won–loss record, but they definitely differ in who we would want working with our own children.

It is always incredible to watch. When someone chooses to yell, and the player or student doesn't do what they want, they often yell again. Only louder the next time. What happens is we have to keep increasing our level of aggression because it did not work the last time. The other thing that happens is that people watching think that is how we are supposed to "coach" young people. One of the most harmful things about watching high-profile, "successful" college-coaches behave that way is that high-school and youth coaches think that that is what coaching is.

The irony is that coaches have incredible power and influence. You can tell the player that if they do not do something specific they will not play again this half. We never have to say it mean, we just have to mean what we say.

I hear parents say, "my child never listens to me." I believe their child listens to every word; the parent just wishes they only listened to some of them. If a parent yells, "You are grounded all summer!" and then says, "Do you want to go get ice cream?" the child listens to it all – they have just learned the parent does not mean what they say.

Other parents never raise their voice to their children. They just mean what they say when they say something. Don't threaten to ground your child all summer unless you are willing to follow through on a credible punishment.

This same thing applies in every classroom. Do not have rules you are not going to continually and consistently enforce. Do not threaten to call parents. Call parents. Do not threaten to hold a student in from recess. Hold them in from recess. We should never say something mean. We just need to make sure we mean whatever it is we say.

20

Every Child Is the Most Precious Thing Imaginable to Their Parents. What If We All Saw in Them the Same Unique Potential That Their Parents See?

There is a mom who is nervous before the school year starts. She is praying that this year will be different. Maybe her son will get a teacher who is able to look past the immaturity and the foolish behavior. Maybe he will get a teacher who sees in him the same potential that she sees. This year, you can be that teacher who is the answer to a mother's prayer.

It was a phone call that I will not soon forget. I had set a goal of making 100 positive phone calls home by the 100th day of school. I asked my teachers to let me know when they had a student they wanted to brag on. One of the teachers emailed me about a student she was proud of. This particular student was always coming to class unprepared. The teacher and student had a "heart-to-heart" conversation, and since then, the student has been bringing her pencil to class every day. I know that coming to class prepared is a big deal, and it can certainly be aggravating to a teacher to always be loaning pencils. Our students, after all, need to be responsible. But I'll admit, I was a bit reluctant to call mom about something as petty as bringing a pencil to class.

I called the student down to my office to give her a high-five, and despite my misgivings, I called mom. I told her how proud her daughter's teacher was of her for bringing a pencil every day. The mom started crying. Through her tears she said, "My daughter struggles in school. Thank you so much for telling me this." I had to end the conversation quickly because I did not want to start crying in front of our sixth grader. I hung up the phone, and the student's eyes were wet too. I could tell she was proud. So this pencil was not petty; it was huge.

This phone call reinforced two important lessons for me: First, teachers have tremendous power to brighten a student's day. And, through a quick phone call to a parent, they can bring some sunshine into their life as well. Do not leave compliments left unsaid. When we are proud of our students, we should tell them.

> **"Do not leave compliments left unsaid."**

When they are making progress, we should encourage them. They will remember our kind words longer than they will remember our lesson. We are not just offering our students an education; we are offering them hope. And second, when we struggle with students, there is a good chance that parents experience those same struggles. There are parents who are nervous every time they put their kids on the bus; they experience a little bit of anxiety every time they drop their children off at school. They are wondering:

"Will he get in trouble again today?"
"Will anyone sit with her at lunch?"

"Will the kids mess with him in the hallway?"
"Will she forget her pencil again?"

There are some students for whom school is not a good experience, and parents share in that struggle with their child. They experience it through the silence in the car, through the constant "stomach aches" in the morning, and sometimes through the very real tears. These students need our attention, they need our patience, and they need our love. Educators make a difference for students every day – and as it turns out, they make a difference for parents too. Parents are grateful when they notice teachers demonstrating genuine care for their kids. Teachers feel like they are just doing their job, but to the parents that "job" is their whole world.

21

Great Teachers Define Their Success by the Success of Their Students. They Understand It's Not About the Teaching, It's About the Learning.

I remember a teacher who would always pester me about when the state test results were coming in. She could not wait to see how her students had done. She spent countless hours tutoring her students and would do anything to help them succeed. She saw the success of her students as a reflection of the work she had done. It has been said, "Until something is learned, nothing is taught." That's a tough adage but great teachers are willing to own it. Several years ago, I remember walking into a teacher's room during his planning period. He was finishing up on the tests he was grading. He looked a little dejected as he remarked to me: "These students all did poorly. Somehow, I didn't communicate the material as well as I thought I had. I'm gonna reteach it and then assess them again." It can be hard for teachers to swallow their pride in those circumstances, but that is what good teachers are willing to do. They understand the bottom line is always student learning, and ensuring student success is what drives them. Good teaching is not just about delivering lessons, it is about being invested in the success of your students. That teacher who could not wait for the scores to come in was not actually "pestering" me. I loved her passion. I loved her commitment. I loved the fact that she was invested in the success of her students.

22

Teachers Who Stay Comfortable Do Not Make Many Mistakes, but They Usually Do Not Innovate Either. If You Want to be Awesome, You Have to Take Risks.

I still remember sitting in a classroom and hearing a teacher tell her students, "I'm nervous about this lesson. I've never done anything like this before." I remember how proud I was of her at that moment. Rarely do I get more excited than when teachers tell me they are trying something new in their classroom. And sometimes they say, "This part didn't work in first period, but I'll tweak it for the rest of my classes." It fires me up when teachers push through some discomfort, when they take those risks, and when they learn through their failures.

My personal journey through discomfort took form as I was confronted with new technology. I found all the changes overwhelming, intimidating, and at times, even scary. I had reluctantly started a Twitter account, so I could connect with other educators, but I still was not sure what some of the functions were. I felt a bit foolish when a friend showed me something simple like how to tag people in a picture. Our system was moving to all things Google, and that was a bit unnerving. I knew a little bit about

PowerPoint, Excel, and Word, and now needed to figure out how to use Docs, Slides, Forms, and Sheets … not to mention a whole new email system. I could not figure out how to store and retrieve all my information on Google Drive. I had just started a blog, and I barely had a clue what I was doing there. I had just started an Instagram account, and my son told me I screwed up my first picture. Yep, it was fair to say that I was uncomfortable.

But here's the thing, I was absolutely certain that I was growing. And I was equally certain that those changes would allow me to be more effective in my job. I made a decision that my commitment to growth must override my desire to stay comfortable. Make no mistake about it, venturing into uncharted waters brings a level of vulnerability. There is some risk that is inherent with any change. It can be challenging, but we must embrace the changes anyway. The risk is worth it.

Imagine the teenager who wants to be a great football player, but he remarks, "I'm just not into lifting weights." Or the aspiring gymnast who says, "Stretching just isn't my thing." It is easy to see how naive, short sighted, and absurd these sentiments are. When people say these sorts of things, we can't take their commitment to their goal seriously. Have you caught yourself saying, "Technology just isn't my cup of tea" or "I see how that's good for some people, but I'm not good at technology?" I know I had said many times, "I'm just not a technology guy."

Well guess what … our students can't afford for us to be average. So we have to jump in head first. It's important to know that this decision is not based on how we feel – because we might

> "Our students can't afford for us to be average. So we have to jump in head first."

be feeling awkward and uncomfortable – we make the decision because we know it is the right thing to do. We may fail. We may fall flat on our face. But that's ok. We never grow if we refuse to step out of our comfort zone. So I'm stepping out. Maybe your goal is not to be THE best, but if you are an educator you know that your work impacts students … and those kids deserve YOUR best.

23

It Is Absolutely Crucial that Teachers Have Fun Teaching. It Is the Only Way the Students Will Ever Have Fun Learning.

When grown-ups sit in boring, unengaging workshops they do not get much out of it. Kids are like small grown-ups – and grown-ups are like big kids. If teachers are not joyful about teaching there is zero chance the students will be joyful about learning. One of the best ways to make students excited about being in your class is to be excited about being their teacher. Good teachers do not just teach lessons, they strive to make coming to school a positive experience for students. They are creating memories for those students. And the students might not remember how much work they put into the class, but they will remember how much heart they put into class. And part of what students find compelling is when their teachers don't try to hide their own humanity. Teachers are not perfect and it works out best when they do not pretend to be. Students love it when their teachers are "real" with them. They love it when teachers don't take themselves too seriously. Students respect the vulnerability, they appreciate the silliness, and they love the humor.

24

Some Students Carry Around the Burden of a Bad Reputation. Be the Teacher Who Gives Them a Fresh Start. Be the Teacher Who Sees in Them the Potential That Their Parents See. YOU Can Be the Teacher that Helps Them "Turn the Corner."

When teachers are looking at rosters before the school year starts, some names may look familiar. They may complain to a colleague, "Oh, I taught his older brother, and he's probably just as bad." Or, "I've heard about her; and I've heard her parents are crazy too!" It is easy for educators to allow reputations and hearsay to shape our opinions and our expectations of the year to come. To be sure, some students have a history of making poor choices, and it would appear that they have earned their "reputation."

I am grateful for the teachers who allow *their* new year to be a new year for their students as well. I appreciate it when teachers ignore the gossip and refuse to accept the prevailing narrative for these students. The high expectations of these teachers allow these students the opportunity to build a new reputation – to write a new story for themselves. Every student deserves that chance. We all make mistakes, and all of us deserve a fresh start ... a shot at redemption. YOU can be that teacher who helps the students "turn the corner."

25

The Most Memorable Lessons Usually Do Not Involve a Textbook.

Students remember collaborating on projects; they remember creating presentations; they remember solving authentic problems; they remember going outside for an activity. They are not likely to remember outlining the chapter, defining the terms in bold, or answering the questions at the end of the section. Face it ... most textbooks are boring. They contain an abundance of information, to be sure, but communicating information shouldn't be the primary goal of educators. We should be creating engaging and memorable learning experiences for our students, and textbooks are usually not the best tool for that.

26

Teachers Should Never Underestimate the Value of "Smiley Faces" on Students' Papers.

Authentic praise never gets old, and a little encouragement can go a long way. Students always appreciate the approval of their teacher. Students who feel validated are generally motivated to work a little bit harder next time. Little gestures from the teacher can communicate to the student: "I'm proud of you!" ... and that reinforcement can be powerful. Good teachers celebrate the baby steps. When students feel validated in their progress, they can be energized to keep trying. And by the

> "Good teachers celebrate the baby steps."

way, I have found that teachers can get excited by little things like stickers too. When I see the reaction of teachers to stickers, I am reminded how much we all value little tokens of appreciation. Everyone needs validation, and everyone appreciates recognition for their efforts.

27

When a Student Is Misbehaving, the Teacher Needs to Make Sure the Student Is the Only One Misbehaving.

It is essential that we treat every student with respect and dignity every day. This is a pretty high standard, but teaching is a pretty high calling. When students are smart alecks, it is so easy to try to top them. We are clever and potentially feel challenged or like we are losing control. And sometimes when we respond inappropriately by yelling or using cutting sarcasm it does work – temporarily. However, the result is a short-term win – and potentially a long-term loss. By treating students – or our own children – in this manner, we are telling them that is how we want them to treat others. We are saying that this is how we hope they behave.

We got into education to be role models. No matter how we act and treat others we are role models. Everyone in your school is a role model. There may be a few people you work with you hope no one is watching, because you know we are all role models – one way or the other.

Students are constantly watching us. Let's make sure we are proud every day of what they see.

28

There Are 101 Ways to Connect with Your Students, but None of Them Work if You Don't Begin with Care – And if You Have That, You Can Make Almost Any Strategy Work.

It is easy to talk about the priority of building relationships with students. Most of us would agree that it is important, but some may not have a good handle on how to go about making it happen. Well the good news is, anyone can make it happen! It starts with a genuine desire to connect with your students. You then spend time talking to them. And I don't mean talking to them about the material you are teaching. Ask them about their family, their friends, their interests outside of school, and maybe even the stuff that aggravates them. You will probably not bond with your students after just one personal conversation. It usually doesn't work that way. Relationships take time. But if you persist with authentic and personal interactions, you will form a connection. Most students appreciate it when their teachers take an interest in them. When they feel like you like them – like you really do care about them – they will usually reciprocate with some positive interactions of their own. But it always starts with the teacher and a genuine care for the students.

29

A 10-Second Conversation with a Student as They Walk into Your Class May Mean More to Them than Your 45-Minute Lesson.

Technology has replaced a lot of things in the classroom. It will never replace a smiling teacher greeting kids as they walk into class. When teachers connect with their students as they enter the room, they engage them in a way that may be more meaningful than the bell ringer. Every time we give a student a high-five, a fist-bump, a handshake, or a hug, we are telling them: "You matter." School is stressful, and it is sometimes hard being a kid. Some students have drama at home, drama on the school bus, and drama in the hallway. When they are able to make a personal connection with the teacher as they walk into class, it can go a long way toward injecting positivity into their day. A genuine greeting at the door can set the tone for the class, it can put the student in a positive frame of mind, and can even change the trajectory of a student's bad day.

30

Not All Your Students Have Hope . . . and When That Fact Hits You, You Realize Your Job Is Bigger than Any Lesson Plan or Standardized Test.

I did not always want to be a teacher. When I began college, my major was sociology. I changed my major to education halfway through my sophomore year after listening to a recording of the 1986 National Teacher of the Year, Guy Doud. In his talk, he shared some of the painful school experiences from his own childhood, as well as the powerful role that a few teachers played in encouraging him and supporting him through school. His poignant talk resonated with me on a visceral level, and I listened to it over and over. This singular tape recording inspired me to become a teacher. I wanted to make a difference too!

As a young teacher working in an inner-city high school, I remember having a discussion with one of my classes about dreams, ambitions, and life goals. I recall one of my sophomores making a comment that caught me off guard. Referring to his own neighborhood, he exclaimed: "I already know I'm going to live here the rest of my life." He said it with a chuckle, and I remember some of the other students laughing. What I took from his comment was that he felt like the rest of the class was talking about pipe dreams – dreams that were unrealistic and unattainable. That was a profoundly sad moment for me. Years later, I ran into a former student from that same school, and in the course of our conversation she underscored the same truth that devastated me as a first-year teacher. Some students do not have hope that their situation can be any different than it is right now. Nobody in their family had ever been to college, so it is unreasonable for them to think that they could go to college. They do not see education as a "way out" because it hasn't helped any of their friends or family get out. This type of mind-set seems to be one of the defining aspects of a culture of poverty.

If you work in an affluent setting, your dynamics might be a bit different, but that doesn't mean that there is more *hope*. You may have students dealing with depression, eating disorders, substance abuse, or anxiety. There are some students who are suffering from emotional neglect at home. They are not lacking for material possessions, but they do not feel loved. There are students who seem to be well off by all appearances, but they are not happy. And they cannot envision circumstances changing in their life to make things any better. They do not see a way out.

As educators, we are not just teaching lessons, we are teaching kids. We want to create brighter futures for our students, but we first need them to envision that brighter future. Teachers have the ability to give students something that is far more valuable

> "Teachers have the ability to give students something that is far more valuable than good grades on a report card. They can give them hope."

than good grades on a report card. They can give them hope. Most students do not realize how much potential they have. That is where teachers come in. They inspire students with possibilities. They instill in them the belief that they can do more than they ever imagined.

31

Treat Every Student with Respect and Dignity Every Day Because We Never Know if This Is the Day that Matters.

Pretty much every teacher chose education because they wanted to make a difference, they wanted to matter. All of us can reflect on an educator who we admired when we were a student. We know how we felt about them. We probably knew how everybody else in that class – and that school – felt about them. We chose education because we want to be that person – that teacher. We want to make that kind of a difference every year and every day to the students we teach. You may have seen the t-shirt that says, "I became a teacher because no one ever asks you who your favorite governor is." Having a significant and lasting impact is one of the many things that makes teachers so special.

Sadly, many people can also recall a teacher who did not make everyone – or even anyone – feel special. Instead of lifting us up they may have put us down. Some of us may have even had a teacher who made students feel less intelligent because of the way they treated them. We all remember these teachers and recall what it felt like to be privy to that class and experience. Sometimes hurt is not a steady drum beat. It may not occur every day or even on a regular basis in a classroom. It may be a one-time lightning strike. Our job as educators is to make sure that we are continually working to lift up students, to make them feel special. All teachers know it. Most teachers do it. And the best teachers do it every day.

32

Good Teachers Understand How to Communicate the Content. Great Teachers Understand How to Connect with Kids.

Good teachers do not just teach lessons, they teach students, and the personal connections they form will always trump the curriculum and the pedagogy. There is not one magical instructional strategy ... but there is magic in connecting with your students. And the best teachers are even relentless about connecting with the more challenging students in their classroom. There is a lot of "whole group" instruction that must happen in a class ... but the individual interactions are often what is most impactful. One-on-one conversations with students can be so powerful.

Teachers can prepare their students for a test without building meaningful relationships with them – but test results are not the only goal of a good teacher. When graduates come back to visit teachers, they visit the ones who took an interest in them. You see, the legacy of great teachers is not usually found in the lessons they taught their students, but in the relationships they built with their students. When teachers are passionate about their lessons, they can transform the learning. In some cases, the personal connections are what actually makes the learning possible.

I learned this lesson as a 22-year-old aspiring teacher, hired to tutor a student in an alternative school for the last few months of the school year. I was supposed to teach a 15-year-old whose behavior and attitude was so severe that he was not able to make it in his regular school. I think it was fair to say that he had been quite challenging to his previous teachers. I do not recall much about our first meeting, but I do remember he came in with what seemed like quite a chip on his shoulder. I think he wore a black t-shirt with the image of a heavy metal band, he had on black combat boots, and his hair was quite unusual to say the least. I quickly figured out that I needed to develop some rapport with this young man or our relationship may never be productive or positive. If I did not make a connection with him, we might both be in for a long couple of months. I found out that he loved music, he loved playing the guitar, and his favorite musician was Alice Cooper. I asked him if he would bring his guitar to school and teach me some chords. I found an old guitar that I could bring, and in between our school work, he started teaching me to play. Sometimes I would practice while he would work. I even learned part of an Alice Cooper song.

The weeks rolled by uneventfully, and he successfully finished his time in the alternative school. There is no doubt in my mind that our time together would not have been nearly as productive if we had not talked about music and not played a little bit of guitar together. More than 25 years later and I still know those guitar chords that he taught me. I think about that experience in the alternative school from time to time, and I am reminded about the importance of connecting with students. The best teachers do not always have the best lessons, but they always have the best relationships with their students. And in some cases, the lessons are not even possible without those relationships.

33

Students Do Not Gravitate to Subjects . . . They Gravitate to Teachers.

When you ask a student what their favorite class is, their answer usually has nothing to do with the subject; it has to do with the teacher. Students may not remember a lesson for a long time, but they will remember some of their teachers forever. They remember the ones who cared, the ones who were silly, the ones who tried to connect with students, the ones who always seemed to love their job. They remember the ones who brought kindness, humor, and joy to the classroom. They remember the teachers who were nice to them.

Any administrator or counselor who has been involved with the course selection process that middle and high-school students go through understands the pivotal role that teachers play in this process. Oftentimes, students will sign up for certain courses simply because of who they know will be teaching them. Students quickly pick up on the reputation of certain teachers. Whether it is picking an elective career tech class, a foreign language course, or challenging themselves with a rigorous Advanced Placement course, students will often make the decision based on who will be teaching it. Students always seem to gravitate to certain teachers. Some things in the school building are not hard to figure out.

34

Teachers Do Not Have to be Funny, but They Do Have to be Fun.

I often ask educators to think of the best teacher they ever had when they were a student. It really livens up the room. You can see on people's faces how remembering what it was like to be a student in that classroom makes them feel special. There is often a sense of excitement that fills the air. What is amazing is the variance between the best teachers. Some were their warm and welcoming kindergarten or first-grade teachers. Others were more content-oriented secondary teachers. For some educators a college instructor or professor had the most significant impact. They cover a wide gamut of ages and fields. Many people recall those who inspired or encouraged them to become teachers themselves.

Then I ask educators to share with a partner or partners what characteristics they would use to describe the best teacher they ever had. At this point the room becomes completely energized. People are smiling, reflecting, and sometimes even tearing up remembering what it was like to be in that classroom with that impactful teacher. There is such a positive feeling as we recall special people and special times.

When the current educators discuss the characteristics of their best teachers, there are many things they seem to have in common. Kind, caring, intelligent, interested in you, challenging, energetic. All of these things are powerful and important. But one thing seems to regularly arise: That is that the best teacher they ever had was fun.

Now when we examine it more closely, fun means different things. A class can be fun because the teacher is funny. Requiring a teacher to be funny probably eliminates a lot of us from being qualified. However, being fun does not. Being able to laugh, laugh at ourselves, smile, and be friendly, are all things that make us fun. Being able to have fun with someone rather than at the expense of someone is an essential element to being a colleague, parent, teacher, or friend. Having a sense of humor is helpful in life, but it is essential in the classroom.

35

Students Need to See Adults Working Successfully Together at School, Otherwise It Is Possible They Will Never See Two Adults Working Together Successfully.

There are so many things schools have to provide students. Safety, security, lunches, financial support, transportation, etc. This is of course in addition to effective instruction. But one thing that we may sometimes overlook is the modeling of relationships. So many students come from non-traditional homes. This is not inherently a negative, nor is it in any way a judgement. However, some home environments can cause limitations in kids' understanding of what functional adult relationships look like. Students need to see this at school, especially if they have not seen this at home.

Many people use the family dynamic they grew up in as a model for normal – whatever normal means. This is obviously a plus if it is a caring and loving household. We also know students that may not have been raised in such a nurturing environment. Instead of coming to school to learn, they may primarily be coming to school to be loved. That is okay. We know that is an essential component of an effective school. However, there is one other essential thing that schools have to provide: Students must have the opportunity to see two adults working successfully together at school. Because too many students – no matter what type of family unit they have – have never seen two adults working successfully together at home.

Think about what an incredible handicap and limitation that is if we allow students to leave our schools without having seen adults working successfully together. Their chances of success at work would be reduced significantly, and their odds of success in a personal relationship may become almost non-existent. Schools must figure out a way to have adults interact so that students can regularly see examples of how people with differing personalities can function in a positive and productive manner. This may just seem like one more thing added to the stack, but it may be one of the more important things to provide our students.

36

Classroom Management Is Not About Having the Right Rules, It Is About Having the Right Relationships.

I have noticed that students behave in some of their classes, and that those same students misbehave in others. I certainly realize that the mix of kids in a classroom can have a big impact on student behavior, but it is still clear to me that teachers are likely to have an even bigger impact on behavior. And usually, the unwritten expectations of the teacher are more important than the rules that are posted on the wall. As it turns out, the first essential step in effective classroom management is actually liking the students in your classroom. Students are so much more responsive to teachers who genuinely like them, and this often translates into better behavior. But the best classroom management is not about controlling behaviour, it's about winning over the kids – building those connections. We earn the respect of our students by how we treat them. We also need to understand that when students act out, it is usually the result of an unmet need. A punishment may address the behavior, but it does not meet the need. Sometimes students need consequences for the misbehavior, but it is not usually the consequences that change the behavior, and very seldom will this win the student over. We do not make connections with consequences; we build them with relationships. It is usually that simple. Classroom management

> "We do not make connections with consequences; we build them with relationships."

is so much easier when you have rapport with the kids. Getting to know your students makes all the difference.

37

Teachers Foster Creativity When They Value Good Questions as Much as They Value Right Answers.

Too often, our schools condition students to "jump through the hoops." Compliance is valued over engagement. Students (and their parents) are often driven by grades rather than being motivated to learn. Many students simply want to know, "Is this going to be on the test?" We need to encourage students to think outside of the norm. We need to value independent thinking and figure out how to capitalize on the questions of students. We begin to encourage innovation when we teach students to recognize that failure presents new opportunities to learn. We encourage it when we validate the effort, not just the result – when we value the process, not just the product.

This process is rarely comfortable for students, but great teachers are able to nudge students out of their comfort zone because of the safe classroom environment they have created. This safe environment is crucial because growth only happens in the context of vulnerability. It only happens when students are comfortable taking risks. One way teachers can create a safe space is to be transparent about their own failures – to be open about the risks they are taking as a teacher. It is important for students to see their teacher make mistakes. It is possible that the most valuable contribution of a teacher might not be found in modelling success, but in modelling the process of working through failure.

38

When a Lesson Does Not Go as Planned, Great Teachers Are Not Looking Around at the Students, They Are Looking in the Mirror.

Every teacher experiences lessons that do not go as planned. The best teachers do not view these lessons as complete failures though, because they learn from them. They do not blame the students – in fact they are not looking to blame anyone. Instead, they are reflecting on their own role in the process. They are thinking about how the objective might have been stated more clearly; they are thinking about a more strategic way to group the students; they are thinking about what activity might have made the topic seem more relevant; they are thinking about how a different assessment at the end of class might have brought more effective closure to the lesson. Great teachers understand their pivotal role in the success of every lesson, and they are continually reflecting on their own practice in order to improve.

39

You Might Never Remember The Most Powerful Conversation You Have with a Student ... But that Student Will.

Teachers have hundreds of interactions with students every day. Many of these conversations are trivial; some of them are more serious. But to a teacher, all of the interactions seem to run together. Oftentimes, at the end of a day, the myriad of conversations with students can seem like a blur. But students usually only interact with a few teachers in the course of their day. It is much more likely that students will remember those conversations than the teacher will. Maybe the teacher is having a hard day and comes across as irritable when they respond. That curt response will leave an impression on the student. Maybe the teacher asked the student about their weekend plans, and the student became excited as they described an upcoming birthday party. There is a chance that the teacher was distracted during the birthday party story. This child's story barely registered on the teacher's radar, but it was a highpoint in the student's day. A lot of things that happen during the school day are insignificant to the adults ... but they can turn into some big memories for the kids. Kind words from a teacher may end up being the highlight of a student's day. We never know what the students will remember, so we need to make all the moments count.

40

When a Great Teacher Is in a Bad Mood, Only One Person Knows. When a Bad Teacher Is in a Bad Mood, the Entire School Knows.

All of us have better days and worse days. No one is at the top of their game every day. However, some teachers somehow seem like they are. They are able to prevent their personal mood from affecting their classroom and their relationships. When a great teacher is in a bad mood they work diligently to keep it from impacting their students and peers. They seemingly magically do not allow it to permeate their teaching.

At the same school there may be other teachers that, when they are in a bad mood, the entire school knows it. Not because it is so noticeable, but because they may even announce it. They sort of use it as a weapon. They may even walk into class in a threatening manner and bark at their students, "Don't try me today! I am in a bad mood!" With a few people this may even be accompanied by a daring glare hoping for pushback.

This does not mean, on those rare occasions, the best teachers do not share with their students that they are not feeling the best, or that something is weighing heavy on their minds or hearts. They just do it with empathy and concern for their students. They do not want to risk the relationships they have worked hard to establish in their classroom.

We all have ups and downs. Some people just work harder at limiting the negative impact on others.

41

Curriculum, Pedagogy, and Technology Have All Changed, But the Qualities of Great Teachers Are – and Always Will Be – Timeless.

If you have taught for a while, you have undoubtedly seen various courses of study come and go. You have seen academic standards change, and then change again. You have experienced the evolution of pedagogy with trends that include cooperative learning, differentiated instruction, and problem based learning. Technological innovations have included everything from mechanical pencils, to film strip projectors, to interactive "smart" boards. Clearly, there is much that changes in education.

But there is one thing that never changes: The qualities of great teachers. The best teachers have three things in common: They are all about the students; they always bring positive energy into the classroom; and they are relentless about getting better. These are qualities that endure. The strategies and practices of educators may change over time, but the core values that inspire great teachers transcend the decades.

42

When Students Leave the Class Feeling Better About Themselves, Their Teacher Understood that There Is More to Teaching than Delivering Instruction.

There is an often quoted adage: "They may forget what you said, but they will never forget how you made them feel." It is often cited by educators because it so poignantly captures the important role that teachers play in creating a positive climate in their classroom. Good teachers are relentless in encouraging their students. They give out compliments on a regular basis. They avoid sarcasm. They control their own negative emotions. Sometimes, teachers may need to infrequently vent to colleagues, but it is never a good idea to disparage their class. Good teachers work to ensure that their class is an emotionally safe place for all their students, and as it turns out, students who feel good about themselves are in a much better position to actually learn something. Students are not overly complicated. They like to feel supported, encouraged, and valued – just like teachers. Here are five tips for building a healthy class climate – the type of class where students leave the room feeling better about themselves:

- ◆ Talk to students when they walk into class.
- ◆ Learn one thing about each student.
- ◆ Praise publicly and criticize privately.
- ◆ Apologize when you need to.
- ◆ Do not take yourself too seriously.

43

Students Love It When Teachers Come to Their Games, Concerts, or Programs. Of Course Teachers Have Their Own Lives Too, but When They Can See Their Students in Action It Means the World to Them.

I remember the evening well. As soon as my daughter got into the car after the volleyball game, she exclaimed, "Dad, my teacher came to my game!" Oftentimes, what students find meaningful about school is the personal connections they have with certain teachers. They always remember the ones that took the time to show an interest in them – to really get to know them. This includes getting to know what they are involved in outside of school. Frankly, what the students are involved in outside of school may be the most important thing to them. It is probably what they are most passionate about. So, when you take the time to show up to a concert, or a play, or a game, it demonstrates that you're trying to enter "their world." The students will notice you, and it will make an impression on them. And more than likely, their parents will notice you as well.

I know that teachers have personal lives, and chances are they may have their own child's events to attend. But when they can find the time to support their students at those extracurricular events, it goes a long way toward developing rapport with the students and generating good will with the parents. When teachers support their students outside the classroom, those students will be more likely to support that teacher inside the classroom.

44

The Best Teachers Never Forgot What It Was Like to Be a Student.

It is hard being a kid, and sometimes it is stressful going to school. It is great when teachers can remember those days – those days when they could not recall their locker combination ... when classmates made fun of their new haircut ... when they were just hoping they would have someone to sit with at lunch. When teachers understand the stresses and anxieties of their students they are more gracious toward them. They have stronger rapport with them.

And sometimes school is boring. The best teachers remember what it was like to watch the clock as the minutes seemed to drag on endlessly. They remember being the only one in the group that was doing all the work. They remember thinking how unfair the teacher seemed for letting students get away with not doing their fair share. This empathy compels these teachers to strive to be a different sort of teacher for their students, and they take this professional responsibility seriously. But they do not take themselves too seriously, because they are still a kid at heart. And students love them for it.

45

Struggling Students Do Not Succeed Because They Are in the Right Class; They Make It because They Have the Right Teacher.

Some students are easy to teach: They are prepared, cooperative, and respectful. But teachers make the most difference with the ones who are hard to teach. Some kids seem to have a hard time behaving, but the right teacher does not give up on them. When a student misbehaves it is not because they like being in trouble. The right teachers get that. They do not lower the bar, but they seek to understand what might be motivating the bad behavior. They show empathy. They build a relationship. They work to help that student feel valued and connected. They believe in that student when others do not.

I will never forget the time that I assigned Erica to the alternative school. She was disruptive, had a bad attitude, and most of the teachers were glad to have her out of the building. But one of her teachers came to me and asked if she could get a pass to walk back to his class for third period. He said, "She has to be there; she can't afford to miss my class." I almost cried when he asked me this.

That is the type of extraordinary compassion and commitment that struggling students need!

There are some students who would not make it through school if not for the patience of certain teachers, the flexibility of certain teachers, and the love of certain teachers.

46

Successful Teachers Start with a Focus on Self. After All, the One Person We Can Most Easily and Effectively Influence Is Ourself.

It is so easy to fall into the "blame game." At times we may hear colleagues talk about the poor job the previous teachers have done preparing the students for us. Maybe the problem is the preschool, possibly it is the elementary school, and of course it could easily be the middle school or junior high. And, heaven knows, with society like it is today, there is plenty of fault with the parents.

Additionally, we may feel that we live where the legislature or the governor acts like they know more than the teachers who have dedicated their lives to positively impacting students. There is plenty of "blame" to go around. And some of these things probably have a piece of truth to them. However, our focus needs to be on what we can control rather than what we cannot control.

As teachers we can decide where to put our time and energy. If we choose to focus on things outside of our immediate influence our efficacy drops significantly. As a result of this, our ability to self-motivate diminishes greatly. It is natural at times to feel frustrated, but it is essential that we do not let these feeling reduce our effort and tone with students.

There are many things that teachers cannot control. Listing them is pretty easy and many teachers' lounges are full of people who do this on a regular basis. However, in order to feel empowered and continue to have the energy needed to make a difference, each of us must regularly recenter on the things we can most impact – ourselves. If you find yourself feeling frustrated with students, not being motivated to go to work, having negative relations with parents and colleagues, there is one thing that we must do to begin the turn around. That is to run in the bathroom and look in the mirror.

We are not alone in our efforts, but the first step has to be a focus on self. Once we recognize that it really is up to us, then we have the potential to find the solution. There are a myriad of resources available, but it is essential to remember that all change starts from within.

47

Being Fair Does Not Mean We Treat Every Student the Same. It Means We Give Each Student What THEY Need. Good Teachers Get that.

Good teachers were accommodating for students long before the Individuals with Disabilities Education Act (IDEA) made Individual Education Plans (IEPs) a legal requirement. They are committed to the success of every student, but they realize that the background, ability, and unique needs of kids have a profound impact on their learning experience. So, good teachers individualize instruction and in some cases individualize assessment. They understand that not every student learns in the same way or at the same rate. Every student deserves a quality education, and that means that some students will be treated differently. Good teachers are committed to the success of every child, so they are willing to do whatever it takes.

48

You Do Not Have to Be Kind to Be a Teacher, but You Do Have to Be Kind to Be a Great One.

There are many qualities of outstanding teachers – engaging, energetic, intelligent, caring, etc. But one that has to be a part of being a difference-maker is being kind. If in doubt, be kind to others. Our students deserve it and our colleagues desire it. When people do not provide this to us it is doubly difficult to dig deep and be kind to them, but that is part of what being a good teacher and a great person is. We all come across way too many students and adults who do not seem to treat others with kindness. And we all come across way too many people who do not treat us with kindness. However, if we do not provide it to them, for many people it is very difficult for them to ever take this approach themselves.

We must always remember that many of our students come from environments that we cannot even imagine. Many of them have never been treated with – or even seen – compassion and caring. If they do not learn it from us they may never learn it. That thought makes us feel sorry for them, but it should shake us to our souls to think what things are going to be like as they raise their own children. Kindness every day is the least we can give our students. They deserve it and so do we.

49

Something that Is Obvious About Good Teachers: They Want to Be Better Teachers.

Most great teachers did not start out that way, and they did not become great by accident. They learned, they adapted, they grew. They did not hide from new ideas, and they were not comfortable with mediocrity. They are committed to being more effective tomorrow than they were today. When the lesson is over, they think about how they can make it better next time. They spend time in the summer thinking about how they can improve their lessons next year. That's just what they do. They do not always have the most innovative lessons, but they keep trying. This relentless commitment to professional growth encourages their colleagues and obviously benefits their students. The teachers that are most admired are not the ones with the best lesson, they are the ones who are always in pursuit of a BETTER lesson.

50

The Best Way to Make Sure Students Do Not Act Like the School Year Is Over Is to Make Sure the Adults Do Not Act Like the School Year Is Over.

School is so interesting because it has such a distinct cycle. There is the excitement of the start of the year, the build up to the different holidays, test time, and, eventually, the end is in sight. Along with the scheduling ups and downs so follows our energy level.

Everyone – students and adults alike – is stoked for the new school year. Hope is prevalent and palpable, optimism reigns, and we all start the new year undefeated. Then behavior issues may crop up, negativity among some of our colleagues might creep in. Certain students challenge our patience and we may even cross paths with a less than positive parent.

There are long stretches between school holidays and the weather may give everyone a little cabin fever. The testing cycle is always in the back of our minds and eventually it is near and then upon us. We feel the crunch of trying to get all of the students prepared and then the concern on eventually finding out the results.

Finally we complete that seemingly crucial task, and when we look up, the end of the year is in sight.

The weather starts to warm up and the students (and teachers) might start to get antsy. At the very least, mentally, we are counting down the days and some classrooms have a number written on the board of school days remaining. Everyone is anticipating the end of the school year. But at this point different teachers head down varying paths.

Some go into stall mode. How can we pass the time each day? Testing is done, the students know whatever we do from this point forward "doesn't count." It is easy for all of us to fall into this same mind-set.

However, some teachers are different. Some realize that any amount of time is precious. All of it can be difference-making. There are teachers that realize since the testing cycle is done they can now do high interest things that are critical to life, just not to the standardized test. This window that remains can open up opportunities that may not be as available at other times of the year.

While some teachers collect books with 10 days left, others are still working to make a difference with 10 minutes left. Our time with students is limited. It is essential that we take advantage of each day to continue to impact the lives of our students.

51

Students Are Much More Likely to Remember What the Adults Are Teaching When the Adults Are Remembering Why They Are Teaching It.

When students ask, "Why do we need to know this stuff?" they are asking a question that deserves a good answer. And teachers need to have a good answer. It really does matter whether teachers believe in what they're teaching. If they are interested in their own lesson, then they will probably be a bit more animated teaching it. If teachers believe that the lesson matters for the students, they will probably work to help students make connections to the material and their own life. If teachers believe that the lesson is truly important, they will probably teach it with a sense of excitement that the students will find compelling. The attitude of the teacher toward the lesson will inevitably affect the passion that the teacher brings to the lesson. And there is little doubt that it will affect the attitude that the students bring to the lesson as well.

52

It Is Important to Catch Kids Being Good – and Recognize Them for It – because Students Need Attention . . . and They Will Get It, One Way or Another.

How often have you heard another teacher complain about a student, saying something like "She's just doing that for attention," or "He's just trying to get the other kids to look at him."? Well ... it is normal to want attention. We all want to be noticed; we all want to matter. When students are getting some attention for the right reasons, they're less likely to seek attention in inappropriate ways. Some kids have good smiles; some ask good questions; some are good at magic; some are creative; some are good helpers; some can remember lines from TV shows; some can make other kids laugh; some have great handwriting. Every kid can do something well! We need to figure out what it is. We need to be relentless about recognizing students for their abilities and contributions – even if they may seem little to us.

53

The Best Thing Teachers Can Do for Their Colleagues Is Bring a Positive Attitude to Work Every Day. Positive Energy Is Contagious.

Your child was up all night with an ear infection; you spilled your coffee on the way to school; the copy machine ran out of toner when you were scrambling to finish your copies for the day. There are a million things that could ruin your day, and sometimes the world seems to be conspiring against you – sapping all your energy and all your joy. There is a picture in my office of Michael Jordan jumping from the free-throw line to dunk a basketball. I added a caption to the picture that reads: "What are YOU rising above?" We cannot always control our circumstances, but we can always control our response to those circumstances. Are you a victim of your circumstances or do you choose to rise above them? And our attitude does not just affect our own emotional well-being, it affects everyone around us. Our attitude is felt at the lunch table, in the hallway, in the workroom, in the faculty meeting, and certainly in our classroom. Good days do not just happen to us; we decide to have good days.

54

We Can Never Change Student Behavior Unless We First Change Adult Behavior.

Every teacher has students they wish behaved better. When someone goes in to observe the very best teachers these dynamic educators seem to have no problems at all. However, that sense of perfection is a fallacy. The best teachers have worked, tweaked, adjusted, and altered their behavior numerous times so that the students would improve the way they behave in the classroom.

We can wish the students have more self-control or had been taught to be more respectful, but often this hope is all for naught. It is funny how the best teachers seem to get the best students every year, but in our hearts we know that it is not a coincidence. We know that what the teacher does is the biggest predictor of what the students do. How the teacher behaves is the biggest impactor of how the students behave.

Centering and reflecting on yourself is the key factor in impacting the students in our classrooms and schools. We should really be relieved by this. If we are waiting for students, parents, or society to change we may be waiting a long, long time. If we are waiting for us to change we can start today.

55

Teachers Do Not Just Make a Difference in Their Classroom, They Make a Difference in the Culture of the School.

When the principal sneezes, the whole school catches a cold. Without a doubt, school culture starts at the top. But while the principal sets the tone for the entire building, no principal creates school culture in a vacuum. School culture is a function of the values, attitudes, and behaviors of ALL the adults in the building. And classrooms are where the magic happens. They are where school culture is built or destroyed. While the most important role for teachers is to *teach* the students in their classroom, they should never underestimate their potential for impacting the culture of the school. Teachers are never neutral with respect to a school's culture. They do things every day that either undermine or enhance the mission of the school. If you are a teacher, here are five concrete ways that teachers positively impact the school's culture:

1. Observe other teachers' classrooms and invite them to observe yours. One of the best professional-development strategies is to learn from the

teachers within your own school. When we initiate peer observations, we foster a culture of collaboration within the building. It creates a more cohesive faculty and increases the likelihood that the best instructional practices in the building get replicated.

2. Take responsibility for your students' academic achievement, and share your data with colleagues. Data are used by the most successful schools to make instructional decisions and drive school improvement efforts. It is not always comfortable to share your assessment results, but it is an essential component of healthy professional learning communities. When you take the potentially scary steps of sharing your data with colleagues, it encourages others to follow suit. Your candor sends the message that weaknesses will be confronted head on. Faculties that are honest with each other about student achievement are in the best position to do something about it. Do not wait on the principal or instructional coach to call a data meeting – you start the conversation. It will make it more likely that your colleagues will share their own data as well.

3. Take risks ... and fail publicly. It is easy for faculties to become complacent, especially when the status quo is adequate. Try something new in your classroom, and let your colleagues know how it goes. If a new activity or strategy does not work out as you hoped, scrap it ... or tweak it, but share your experiences and move on. Your courage and your transparency will inspire other teachers to break out of their own ruts. Innovation thrives in schools where teachers are free to fail.

4. Be patient with the most challenging students … and never lose sight of your purpose. Most teachers have some difficult students at some point

> "Be patient with the most challenging students … and never lose sight of your purpose."

during the day. It can be tempting for teachers to complain about them in the lounge, at the lunch table, in the hallways, or even at faculty meetings. You have to teach the reluctant learners also, but we need to give them the benefit of the doubt. Show empathy and understand that the inappropriate behaviors are a manifestation of dysfunctional circumstances outside of school that we hope no student has to deal with. Your attitude toward the toughest students will not go unnoticed by other teachers. It is usually the case that the most difficult kids need the most TLC. Your patience with these students reminds other teachers what is really important – making a difference in the lives of kids.

5. Stay positive … even in the face of adversity. We all have tough days, and some circumstances seem to conspire to destroy the morale of the faculty. Smile, remain optimistic, and figure out a way to remind your colleagues "the glass is half full." Optimism is contagious. So is pessimism. Which one do we want to permeate the school? The positive energy you bring to work each day will lift the spirits of those around you. Your commitment to maintaining a positive outlook will generate positive energy in the building that can make the naysayers irrelevant.

If you're a teacher, it's in your DNA to make a difference!
You are hardwired for significance. You are usually
aware of the difference you make with kids; but never
forget the difference you make with adults. You say and
do things on a daily basis that transcend your classroom
and shape the culture of your school. The values, attitudes,
and behaviors that you bring to work can inspire your
colleagues, they can reinforce the core values of the school,
and they can enhance the collective efforts of all those in
the building who are working to make the school's vision
a reality. Remember: Peer pressure does not end with
adolescence.

56

Teachers Leave a Legacy that Transcends the Lesson Plans, the Letter Grades, and the Test Scores.

If you are a teacher, you have taught (or will teach) hundreds of kids. You are a professional, and you are creating a legacy every day that you come to work. You are leaving your mark – an indelible impression upon the children entrusted to your care. What will they remember about you I wonder ...

> *They may not remember your tier-two interventions.*
> *They may not remember your authentic assessments.*
> *They may not remember your brilliantly scaffolded lessons.*
> *They may not remember your innovative rubrics.*
> *They may not remember your curriculum map.*
> *They may not remember how cute your bulletin boards were.*
> *They may not remember their benchmark scores.*
> *They may not remember that you always had your objectives written on the board.*
> *They may not remember your bell-ringers or your exit slips.*

They may not remember how many degrees you had or that you were "highly qualified."

These are all good things, and teachers are more effective when their professional practice reflects the qualities and behaviors on this list. The fact that your students may not remember these things could discourage you. Do not let it. There are plenty of things that your students will remember.

They will remember that time you played dodgeball with them in PE.

They will remember the fist-bumps every time they walked into your class.

They will remember the funny stories you told about your vacation.

They will remember those times you never gave up on them.

They will remember how kind you were.

They will remember that you had real conversations with them in the hallway.

They will remember that time you intervened with the students being mean in the lunchroom.

They will remember that you always had a smile.

They will remember that time you made a bad decision . . . but you apologized to the entire class.

They will remember that time they forgot their lunch, but you made sure they ate.

They will remember you coming to their games and concerts.

They will remember that you always seemed to be excited about teaching.

They will remember that you didn't mind being silly.

*They will remember the time you called them at home
when they were sick.*

*They will remember that you seemed to genuinely enjoy
being around students.*

*They will remember that you were patient . . . even with
those who did not always deserve it.*

*They will remember that there were days that you made
school bearable for them.*

They will remember that you encouraged their dream.

Continue to engage in all those activities and strategies that characterize professional educators. The conscientious practice of your craft will elevate the academic achievement of your students and contribute toward making their future brighter. But remember that you are leaving a legacy that transcends grades and test scores. Your impact on kids will be felt in the little moments – the handshakes, the high-fives, the hugs, and the quiet conversations. Do not forfeit any of those moments; your kids will remember them.

So your students will remember you, and they will smile – because you were their teacher, and YOU made a difference!

Continue the Conversation

Which truths and anecdotes resonated with you the most? Share your thoughts and join the conversation with Danny Steele (@steelethoughts) and Todd Whitaker (@toddwhitaker) on Twitter using the hashtag #essentialtruths.